THE THREE AGES

CAMBRIDGE
UNIVERSITY PRESS

University Printing House, Cambridge CB2 8BS, United Kingdom

Published in the United States of America by Cambridge University Press, New York

Cambridge University Press is part of the University of Cambridge.

It furthers the University's mission by disseminating knowledge in the pursuit of
education, learning and research at the highest international levels of excellence.

www.cambridge.org
Information on this title: www.cambridge.org/9781107662612

© Cambridge University Press 1943

First published 1943
First paperback edition 2014

A catalogue record for this publication is available from the British Library

ISBN 978-1-107-66261-2 Paperback

THE THREE AGES

An Essay
on
Archaeological Method

BY

GLYN E. DANIEL, M.A., Ph.D.

of the Faculty of Archaeology and Anthropology
and Fellow of St John's College,
Cambridge

CAMBRIDGE
AT THE UNIVERSITY PRESS
1943

NOTE

My thanks are due to

Professor D. A. E. Garrod, Miss M. M. O'Reilly,
Mrs Leslie Murray-Threipland, and Mr O. G. S. Crawford
for their kindness in reading through this article and
making many helpful and valuable criticisms, and to
the Reverend M. P. Charlesworth and Miss O'Reilly for
reading the proofs.

GLYN E. DANIEL

NEW DELHI,
April 1943

THE THREE AGES

IT is just over a hundred years since the first scientific formulation of a concept—the concept of the three technological ages of man—which Joseph Déchelette described as 'the basis of prehistory'[1] and which Professor R. A. S. Macalister called 'the corner-stone of modern Archaeology',[2] for it was in 1836 that Christian Jürgensen Thomsen published, in his preface to a Guide-book,[3] his division of human history, on the basis of the raw materials of industry, into three ages—the Stone Age, the Bronze Age, and the Iron Age. A century of archaeological discovery and research has changed the use and modified the significance of this concept. 'While', to quote Professor Fleure, 'we are permanently indebted to the archaeologists who first made a chronological scheme of Old Stone, New Stone, Bronze, and Early Iron Ages, we are getting beyond that classification as some of the pioneers foresaw that we should.'[4] It is the object of this paper briefly to describe the origins and development of the idea

[1] *Manuel d'archéologie préhistorique* (1908), I, p. 11.
[2] *Textbook of European Archaeology* (1921), I, p. 11.
[3] *Ledetraad til Nordisk Oldkyndighed* (Copenhagen, 1836); the preface is not signed. A German edition of the Guide appeared in 1837 under the title of *Leitfaden zur nordischen Alterthumskunde*; an English translation by Lord Ellesmere in 1848 entitled *A Guide to Northern Antiquities*. Thomsen develops his ideas in his *Skandinaviska Nordens Urinvånare* (1838–43); second edition 1862–6.
[4] *Arch. Camb.* 1924, p. 241.

of the three ages, and to discuss some of the aspects of its applicability to the modern study of prehistoric archaeology.[1]

I

The story of Thomsen's life and work has often been well and fully told.[2] In 1806, a Commission was appointed by the Danish Government to investigate scientifically the geology and the natural and human history of Denmark. One of the Commission's many problems concerned the Danish burial chambers and kitchen-middens; and Professor Rasmus Nyerup, its secretary, made extensive collections of antiquities from these ancient sites and from the Danish bogs. These and other collections formed the nucleus of a museum in Copenhagen. In 1816, Thomsen succeeded Nyerup as secretary of the Commission and was, at the same time, appointed the first curator of the newly-formed National Museum, a post which he held until his death in 1865. Thomsen's first task was to arrange

[1] Professor Childe discusses the modern applications of Thomsen's three ages in his Presidential Address to the Prehistoric Society (*Proc. Preh. Soc.* 1935, pp. 1 ff.), and I am much indebted to this brilliant and scholarly study of prehistoric methodology.

[2] See especially Moritz Hoernes, *Geschichte und Kritik des Systems der drei prähistorischen Culturperioden* (*Mittheilungen der Anthropologischen Gesellschaft in Wien*, Sitzungsberichte, 1893, pp. 71–8); Reinach, *L'Anthropologie*, 1893, pp. 476–84 (a summary of Hoernes); Hugo Mötefindt, 'Das Dreiperiodensystem', *Mannus*, II, 294–308; Beltz in Ebert, *Reallexikon der Vorgeschichte*, s.v. Dreiperiodensystem; Seger, 'Die Anfänge des Dreiperioden-Systems', in the *Schumacher Festschrift* (Mainz, 1930).

the collections in his museum. Nyerup, who had been collecting and studying northern antiquities for many years, and who has been described as 'the most eminent archaeologist of his time in Denmark',[1] had been unable to introduce any order into the collections, and indeed confessed that 'everything which has come down to us from heathendom is wrapped in a thick fog; it belongs to a space of time which we cannot measure. We know that it is older than Christendom, but whether by a couple of years, or by a couple of centuries, or even by more than a millennium, we can do no more than guess.'[2] Nyerup's attitude was typical of informed opinion all over northern Europe before the formulation of Thomsen's concept.[3] All the prehistoric antiquities were grouped together, and the few literary references that could be gleaned from early histories and sagas and from old traditions were eagerly applied to them all. In Britain, for instance, it was customary to describe all the most ancient monuments and portable antiquities which had no place in written history as Celtic or Druidic or Pictish or by other names derived from Caesar and Tacitus. This was because archaeologists believed with Dr Johnson that 'All that is really known of the ancient state of Britain is contained in a few pages.

[1] Macalister, *op. cit.* p. 9.
[2] *Oversyn over Fædernelandets Mindesmærker fra Oldtiden*, quoted by Sophus Muller, *Nordische Altertumskunde* (Strassburg, 1897), I, p. 218; the translation quoted here is from Macalister, *op. cit.* p. 9.
[3] And, alas, uninformed and conservative opinion for a long time afterwards. Who has not come across museum specimens labelled 'Ancient British' in a delightful non-committal way?

We can know no more than what old writers have told us.'[1] It was Thomsen who, with his concept of the three ages, first introduced some form of classification and some semblance of order into the study of prehistoric remains and began to show that we can know more 'than what old writers have told us'.

Thomsen arranged the specimens in his museum and classified them on the basis of the material used in making weapons and implements—especially cutting tools such as axes and knives—and on this basis he divided his museum collections into three groups representing what he claimed were three chronologically successive ages of stone, bronze, and iron. As Déchelette insisted,[2] Thomsen's concept was first and foremost a museum classification. This arrangement of the museum and the postulation of the three ages was of the greatest value, for, in the first place, it provided a basis for prehistoric systematisation—a basis which would have been valuable even if it subsequently was proved to be incorrect; it produced some kind of order out of the chaos of Ancient Britons and Iberians and Druids and Germans which had hitherto represented the pre-Roman period in northern Europe. Secondly, it was a generalisation made by scientific deduction about the industrial progress of man which all subsequent research has shown to be, for the greater part, true. There is no doubt in my mind that Thomsen's work on the three ages

[1] For a good account of Johnson's disputes with Lord James Burnett Monboddo see Casson, *The Discovery of Man* (1939), pp. 164–6.
[2] *Op. cit.* pp. 11–12.

is the first and most important advance in prehistoric research in the nineteenth century; as Déchelette declared, it marks 'une date dans les annales de la science'.[1] Thomsen himself realised that the formulation of this concept was the most important scientific contribution of his life; and he showed this in an amusing way, as Hermansen notes,[2] by bearing as his coat of arms a shield blazoned in three colours—grey to represent the Stone Age, bronze for the Bronze Age, and black for the Iron Age.

Thomsen's idea was based on an analysis of large quantities of prehistoric antiquities, but even so it was still only a plausible theory of the progress of human industrial development: it was still, as Macalister says, 'nothing more than a working hypothesis'.[3] Thomsen's pupil (who later succeeded him in 1865 as curator of the museum at Copenhagen), Jan Jakob Asmussen Worsaae, however, demonstrated stratigraphically in the Danish peat-bogs that these three ages were distinct entities, and that they succeeded each other in the order that Thomsen suggested. Worsaae has been called 'the founder of comparative prehistoric archaeology',[4] and it was his work and that of other contemporary Scandinavian archaeologists such as Sven Nilsson, Japetus Steenstrup, and Forchhammer that proved beyond all cavil that Thomsen's hypothetical three ages were, at least in northern Europe, historical facts and not merely classificatory abstractions.

[1] *Op. cit.* p. 11.
[2] *Aarbøger for Nordisk Oldkyndighed og Historie*, 1934, p. 99.
[3] *Op. cit.* p. 10.   [4] Hoernes, *op. cit.* p. 72.

The concept of the three ages spread rapidly among the archaeologists and historians of other parts of Europe; the works of Thomsen, Worsaae, and Nilsson were widely translated. Lord Avebury translated into English one of Nilsson's books,[1] and himself wrote a book called *Prehistoric Times*,[2] which introduced to the English reading public the three-age system. Wherever in Europe the three-period system was applied, it was found to agree with the evidence of archaeology and excavation: by the middle of the nineteenth century there were few serious antiquaries who doubted that in Europe and the Near East there had been in prehistoric times three chronologically successive stages in the industrial evolution of man.

Certainly there were some doubters: it would have been very surprising if there had not been, and if the system had not met with some opposition. The idea of an age when only bronze and stone tools, and no iron ones, existed, was especially attacked in many areas. Christian Hostman and Ludwig Lindenschmidt[3] in Germany, and James Fergusson in England,[4] criticised severely the concept of the Bronze Age. Indeed Hostman declared that

[1] Sven Nilsson, *The Primitive Inhabitants of Scandinavia* (edited by Avebury), 1868.

[2] First published in 1865. New editions from 1865 to 1913 (the 7th). See also his *Origins of Civilisation* (first published 1870).

[3] Hostman, 'Zur geschichte und kritik des nordischen Systemes der drei Kulturperioden', *Archiv für Anthrop.* III (1875): republished in 1890 as *Studien zur vorgeschichtlichten Archaeologie*, with a foreword by Lindenschmidt.

[4] See his *Rude Stone Monuments* (London, 1872).

no Stone Age had existed either, and that the finds attributed to the Bronze Age were really those of the pre-Roman and Roman iron ages. But the attackers of the Thomsen system did not attract a great following, and the system soon became the fact of prehistory.

Although, as we have already mentioned, Thomsen did not publish his three-age system until 1836,[1] he had devised the concept soon after his appointment as secretary and curator, if not before. The reports of the Commission for 1818 and 1820 refer to Thomsen's 'new arrangement' of the museum,[2] a letter which has recently been discovered from Thomsen to a Swedish scholar, dated July 1818,[3] refers to these arrangements, an entry for September 1820 in Professor Paulsen's diary refers to Thomsen's classification,[2] and in 1824 Thomsen is defending his system in a correspondence with Dr Büsching,[4] who had denied the chronological succession of these ages. It is clear then that the genesis of the scientific formulation by Thomsen of the three-age system dates from the second decade of the nineteenth century, even if its first publication by him does not antedate 1836.

[1] Adolf Michaelis (*A Century of Archaeological Discoveries* (1908), pp. 209, 343) unaccountably gives this date as 1832.

[2] Victor Hermansen, C. J. Thomsens Første Museumsordning, *Aarbøger for Nordisk Oldkyndighed og Historie*, 1935, pp. 99–122 (with French résumé). See this article for the dating of the development of Thomsen's ideas.

[3] To be published by Bengt Hildebrand.

[4] See Dr Büsching's book, *Abriss der deutschen Alterthumskunde* (Vienna, 1824) and the discussion by Seger, *op. cit.* and Hermansen, *op. cit.*

It has sometimes been claimed that other archaeologists had a share in the first scientific formulation of the system. Friedrich Lisch was in 1836 appointed curator of the Grand-Duke of Mecklenburg-Schwerin's museum in Ludwigslust Castle, and began to classify the collections on the three-age system. He continued a publication begun by his predecessor and called *Frederico-Francisceum*, and in an issue dated 1837 he sets forth the three-age system.[1] Lisch does seem to have hit upon the three-age system independently of Thomsen, but his exposition of it was not as detailed nor as clear as that of Thomsen and he cannot claim priority for its discovery, for, as we have seen, Thomsen had evolved the idea in the second decade of the nineteenth century. Danneil, working on the prehistoric graves in the Salzwedel, seems to have hit upon the idea of the three ages at much the same time as Lisch.[2] Lowie[3] follows Undset[4] in according to the Danish historian Vedel-Simonsen the honour of first proposing the three ages, but it was certainly Thomsen who first put forward the system on empirical grounds, and in any case, whether the idea was first conceived by Thomsen or by Vedel-Simonsen or Lisch or Danneil, there is no doubt that it was the work of Thomsen and Worsaae that diffused the idea throughout Europe.

The phrase 'scientific formulation' has been used ad-

[1] Hoernes, *op. cit.* .p. 72.

[2] On Danneil's work see Mötefindt, *op. cit. supra*.

[3] *History of Ethnological Theory* (1937), p. 21.

[4] *Revue d'Anthropologie*, 1887, pp. 313 ff. On Vedel-Simonsen see also Hoernes, *op. cit.* p. 72.

visedly in discussing the part played by Thomsen in the origin of the three-age system, for, as with so many modern scientific and philosophic concepts, the idea of the three ages was not unknown to the ancient Greek and Roman writers. Thus Lucretius (98–55 B.C.) in his work, *De Rerum Natura*,[1] contends that man first used his nails and teeth, and stones and wood and fire, and then later copper, and then still later iron gained in popularity.[2] Of course, this was just a general scheme of the development of civilisation and was based entirely on abstract speculation: the Greeks had many other 'ages' which they postulated—the Age of Reason, the Golden Age, the Heroic Age. Nevertheless, for all its speculative character, Lucretius's analysis was a very shrewd guess at what had actually been the industrial development of early man in Europe.

There was no clear statement of the notion of the three

[1] See especially Book v, lines 922–1457. The following oft-quoted lines (1283 ff.) summarise his ideas:

> 'arma antiqua manus ungues dentesque fuerunt
> et lapides et item silvarum fragmina rami,
> et flamma atque ignes, postquam sunt cognita primum.
> posterius ferri vis est aerisque reperta.
> et prior aeris erat quam ferri cognitus usus,
> quo facilis magis est natura et copia maior.'

[2] On Lucretius's three-age notions see Penniman, *A Hundred Years of Anthropology*, p. 35. Hesiod expressed in the eighth century B.C. similar ideas to those of Lucretius (see *Works and Days*, l. 150) and spoke of a period when bronze had not been superseded by iron. Pausanias (writing about A.D. 170) declares that in Homeric times all weapons were of bronze (III, 3⁸).

ages between Lucretius and Thomsen in 1836, although some writers in the eighteenth century seem vaguely to anticipate Thomsen. Rhind,[1] de Mortillet,[2] and Evans[3] have drawn attention to some of these eighteenth-century writers: they include Professor Iselin of Basle, Professor Eckard in Germany, Mahudel and Goguet in France, Pennant, Dr William Borlase, Littleton, and Sir Richard Colt Hoare in England. Rhind goes so far as to declare that Thomsen was not the originator of the three-age system but merely the first to give it practical effect.[4] It is no doubt true that in the writings of some of these eighteenth-century scholars we may detect the idea of former ages of stone and bronze and iron in the prehistoric past, but these writings, like those of Hesiod and Lucretius, are based on abstract speculations. We repeat: it was Thomsen who first induced scientifically the existence of these ages, and Worsaae who first proved them empirically. It is to these Scandinavian archaeologists that we must ascribe, as Lord Avebury has said, 'the merit of having raised these suggestions to the rank of a scientific classification'.[5]

Goldenweiser, in his masterly critique of the development and limitations of the comparative method,[6] regards the theory of the three technological ages merely as an

[1] *Arch. Journ.* 1856, pp. 208–14.   [2] *Le Préhistorique* (1901), Chap. II.
[3] *Ancient Stone Implements of Great Britain* (1897), pp. 3–4.
[4] *Op. cit.* p. 211.   [5] *Prehistoric Times*, 7th ed. (1913), p. 6.
[6] *Anthropology: An Introduction to Primitive Culture* (New York, 1937), Chaps. XXX and XXXI, 'Evolution and Progress'. On the three ages see especially p. 510 and pp. 513–14.

application to the field of technology of the evolutionary schemes which nineteenth-century anthropologists, sociologists, and historians were devising in all branches of human culture: the three technological ages would thus have originated in the same way as the famous three economic stages of man,[1] the stages in religious evolution propounded by Spencer, Tylor, and Jevons, and those in social organisation devised by Bachofen, McLennan, and Morgan.[2] But this view, though attractive, is historically inaccurate: the theory of the three ages preceded the application to human problems of the ideas of the classical evolutionists, for Thomsen was contemporary with Lamarck, von Baer, and Lyell, and before Darwin and Spencer. It was not developed by observing existing human communities in various technological stages and arranging these observed stages in a hypothetical order dictated by evolutionary dogma[3]—the Stone Age, as the most remote from modern man, being therefore the earliest, and the Iron Age, in which we are still living,

---

[1] Hunting and fishing, pastoralism, agriculture: these three economic stages are not to be confused with the technological stages nor with Elliott Smith's distinction between food-gathering and food-producing communities nor with Childe's functional-economic system.

[2] All these systems have been disproved. The breakdown of the three-age system in Africa and Polynesia (on which see *infra*, p. 23) is no indictment of the comparative method, as Goldenweiser argues (*op. cit.* pp. 513–14).

[3] Auguste Comte admittedly adopted this point in a general way and argued that existing living peoples revealed all stages through which man has passed in his evolution.

being the most recent.[1] The concept of the three ages was, we repeat, first a hypothesis of Thomsen's based on an analysis of the Danish prehistoric material: and secondly, a fact proved empirically by Worsaae's excavations. I have no doubt that the spread of the idea of these three technological stages was in large measure due to the preoccupation of nineteenth-century anthropologists with ideas of social evolution and to their predisposition towards schemes which showed man everywhere to be 'progressing'. But the roots of the theory of these technological stages is not to be found in the social evolutionary hypothesis of the comparative methodologists: the roots are in the facts of Danish prehistory. And unlike the social evolutionary schemes, the technological scheme was a fact—a proved hypothesis: from the early nineteenth century the theory of the three ages became the fact of the three ages.

II

We have now discussed briefly the genesis and spread of the Thomsen theory of the three ages and declared it to be the fact of nineteenth-century prehistory. What exactly is this fact? The notion behind the three-age system is essentially a very simple one: it is just that in the industrial development of man in Europe there were three successive ages: the first—the Stone Age—in which he used stone for the manufacture of his tools and weapons and knew no

[1] Perhaps it could be said with some justice that we no longer live in the Iron Age or even in a Steel Age but in an age of power-tools.

metal; a second—the Bronze Age—in which he used metal, but only copper and bronze, and had not yet learnt the use of iron; and a third—the Iron Age—in which we are still existing at the present moment in Britain,[1] and in which iron was used in the manufacture of tools and weapons. Many of the early archaeologists realised clearly the implications and limitations of this concept. They realised, in the first place, that there was a considerable overlap between the three ages, i.e. that the transition from Stone Age to Bronze Age and from Bronze Age to Iron Age was not sudden and sharp, that no hard and fast lines could be drawn between the periods, that they merged into each other and that there were transition phases—in short, that each new age was not heralded by a cataclysm. 'Like the three principal colours of the rainbow', said Evans, 'these three stages of civilisation overlap, intermingle, and shade off the one into the other.'[2] 'These three ages must necessarily overlap', declared Boyd Dawkins, 'they cannot reasonably be viewed as hard and fast lines of division.'[3]

Further, the concept of the three ages did not necessarily imply that only bronze was used in the Bronze Age and only iron in the Iron Age and nothing but stone in the Stone Age. The pioneers of the idea appreciated that there was another kind of overlap between the three ages, and that stone did not go out of fashion at the beginning of the Bronze Age, and that the advent of iron did not mean

[1] See footnote on page 16.   [2] *Op. cit.* p. 2.
[3] *Cave Hunting* (1874), p. 139.

the end of bronze. Stone finds are common in bronze and iron age contexts and, indeed, up to the present day stone implements are used as whetstones and gunflints and strike-a-lights. Indeed, in some cases it may be that bronze tools are less frequent in Bronze Age layers than are stone tools, and that in deposits dating to the Iron Age far more tools of bronze and stone occur than those of iron.

The early archaeologists appreciated, too, that artefacts of wood and bone and clay might have been and were used at various times in human development, and they conceded too that the three ages might not represent the whole development of human industry as expressed in terms of its dominant materials. It will be remembered that Lucretius himself supposed that there may have been a period in man's history prior to the age of stone when bone or wood was used, and of which, from the very nature of things, we have little evidence.[1] Von den Steinen described some South American natives who, though not possessing a knowledge of metal, yet cannot be described as being in the Stone Age for they lack stone and their tools are made entirely of shell, wood, bone, and other similar materials.[2]

It was soon appreciated, too, that the presence of a stray object of copper or bronze does not constitute a Bronze

---

[1] Menghin's notion of bone cultures contemporary with the flake- and core-civilisations of the early Pleistocene should be noted here (see *Weltgeschichte der Steinzeit, passim*).

[2] *Unter den Naturvölkern Zentral-Brasiliens* (Berlin, 1897), p. 196.

Age, nor a single iron tool an Iron Age: bronze and iron have clearly to be a basic part of the economy of the people concerned before they can be described as being in a Bronze Age or Iron Age. As Professor Childe says, 'a few objects of copper and bronze or imitations of such in stone need not mark the beginning of the Bronze Age: we have to consider the whole habit of the culture in which they were imported and the manner in which the metal is employed.'[1] Indeed, before a people can properly be said to be in, say, the Iron Age, they must not only be extensively equipped with iron tools and weapons, but they must surely have knowledge of the smelting and alloying of ores and, if not this, at least of the working of metal objects. Childe draws attention to the economy of the Pacific Islands natives when they first came into contact with Europeans: they possessed iron tools but had no idea how they were made. As Childe remarks, 'It would be absurd to describe such native cultures as Iron Age';[2] they were Stone Age cultures—to them metal was merely a superior kind of stone. Bragg notes that when the Eskimos of Baffin Bay were discovered in 1818 they had iron knives made of pieces detached from a meteorite, but had no notion of metallurgy and were strictly in the Stone Age.[3]

Some of the early archaeologists also realised that in any given community the poorer classes might be unable to

[1] *Proc. Preh. Soc.* 1935, p. 9.
[2] *Ibid.* See also *Journ. Roy. Anth. Inst.* LXII, p. 1.
[3] W. H. Bragg, *Old Trades and New Knowledge* (1926).

procure the metals used by the more wealthy folk in the manufacture of their tools and implements and that such social and economic factors as these might conspire to produce local stone ages among the Bronze Age: Boyd Dawkins realised the possibility of these social and personal differences.[1] Evans also fully realised that the sequence of ages was not always fully represented in every European community, and that some people might proceed from an age of stone to one of iron.

What the concept of the three ages implies then, with these modifications, is that, as soon as we can recognise tools made by man in prehistoric Europe, as soon as we can identify man's first extra-corporeal limbs, we find them to be of worked stone: this is the first stage of human industrial development in Europe, and man is described as being in the Stone Age—he uses tools of stone and bone and wood—but principally stone—and no metal. Then he discovers metal and uses first copper and then bronze, although also still using his former tools: then gradually the knowledge of iron is diffused and he uses iron, bronze and stone tools and is in the third and last stage—the Iron Age.

Other implications have been read into the three-age system. It has been argued that if they were not cataclysmic in character at least they were economic revolutions and mark more than technological changes: it has been claimed they mark economic phases. Childe has argued eloquently the social and economic implications of

[1] Conservatism and monopoly might produce similar effects.

metallurgy. A stone axe, he argued, can be fashioned by anybody in a group of hunters and peasants: 'It implies neither specialisation of labour nor trade beyond the group';[1] but the bronze axe is a superior implement in that it presupposes 'a more complex economic and social structure';[1] it implies trade, communications, imported substances, surplus for barter, specialists for casting bronze with a knowledge of geology, chemistry, and a mastery of complex technical processes. Again Childe stresses the economic and sociological implications of the Iron Age: 'Iron tools', he says, 'were much cheaper and could, therefore, be very widely distributed and used extensively for clearing forests and draining marshes.'[2] Indeed, Childe sees very vast changes implied by these technological stages and makes them of the very greatest importance in human history.[3]

Professor Fleure, on the other hand, does not agree with the great economic significance attributed to Thomsen's technological stages. 'The changes suggested by the above names are not everywhere first-class revolutions', he says,[4] and again, 'nearly every student of Brittany is agreed', he declares, 'that...the coming of metal does not make a conspicuous revolution'.[5] In any case, Fleure continues, the introduction of bronze does not work a revolution for

[1] *Man Makes Himself* (1936), p. 9. [2] *Ibid.* pp. 41, 258.
[3] Childe declares that the innate superiority of bronze axes over stone axes and of iron ones over bronze has been over-emphasised: their significant superiority, he claims, lies in the social implications of bronze axes and the cheapness of iron tools.
[4] *Arch. Camb.* 1924, p. 241. [5] *Ibid.* 1924, p. 244.

a long time: first there is a general infiltration of metal so that if there were these economic changes they would not coincide with the technological stages. Ischer insisted that the introduction of metal brought no economic revolution to the Swiss lake-dwellings.[1]

I remain very dubious of the economic changes which are alleged to come immediately in the wake of the technological stages, and it is certainly worth noting that both trade and economic specialisation existed in the Stone Age.[2] That these technological stages had economic implications is indisputable, but these economic changes are not the chief characteristics of these stages, and far more vital economic changes cut across the division into the three ages. Thus one of the greatest breaks in human history, the change from Food-Gathering to Food-Producing, took place during the Stone Age in Europe and the Near East, and in central and northern Europe fundamental economic changes are associated not with the beginning of the Bronze Age but with the beginning of the Late Bronze Age.[3]

Such then, with its limitations, was Thomsen's scheme of the three ages. We must emphasise here that in its genesis Thomsen meant it to apply to Scandinavia and the surrounding regions: unlike the scheme in the *De Rerum*

[1] 'Chronologie des Neolithikums der Pfahlbauten der Schweiz', *Anz. für schweiz. Alterthumskunde*, 1919, pp. 129–154.
[2] Childe admits this but says the trade was not extensive nor fundamental to Stone Age culture: but cf. the flint mine.
[3] On the economic changes see *infra*, p. 45.

Natura it was not at first intended to account for the development of all peoples all over the world. But it has frequently been employed in a world-wide sense, and here its validity breaks down. The people in Oceania proceeded straight from a Stone Age to an Iron Age, and, as Seligman has recently reminded us,[1] there was no Bronze Age in Africa. The Thomsen system is only of world-wide applicability in that everywhere the archaeological record reveals man first as a stone-user, as living in the Stone Age.[2] For the rest, the development through a Bronze Age into an Iron Age only applied to Europe, the Near East, and Asia. Thomsen's three ages are technological stages in the development of man in a portion only of the Old World.

The nature of these stages must not be misunderstood any more than their geographical limitations. I think many early archaeologists were free from some illusions about the three-age system which later archaeologists entertained and still entertain. They had no illusions about the genesis and spread of these ages. Latterly, however, it has been suggested that the three ages are 'natural developments'. Professor Peet held this view and, writing of the three ages, declared, 'these are natural stages in a rational development'.[3] There seems no good reason to support this view: the spread of the various ages depended on the spread of traders or smiths with

[1] *Races of Africa* (1939), p. 156.
[2] But see the views of von den Steinen and Menghin quoted *supra*, p. 18.　　　[3] *Liverpool Annals Arch. Anth.* 1913, V, p. 113.

metal tools and of metal-using peoples; and it has been conditioned, too, by a nearness to supplies of metal, or by the possibility of getting metal supplies by trade. There are many communities who, from isolation and other causes, have not advanced to a metal age, however natural and rational and desirable such a development might seem.

There are other limitations on the implications and universality of the concept of the three ages which the early nineteenth-century archaeologists were not so ready to appreciate. They did not realise that not only was it possible for communities to proceed directly from a stone-using economy to one of iron, but that it was possible for the succession of stages to be reversed, i.e. for metal-using communities to develop into non-metal-using communities, and for a Stone Age to succeed the Bronze Age or Iron Age. Students of material culture are familiar with the decay of useful arts, and the art of metallurgy is sometimes one of these lost arts. The communities who diffused the prehistoric burial chambers along the coasts of Atlantic Europe used metal tools in their South Iberian homes, but metal occurs so very rarely in primary contexts in British or Scandinavian megalithic tombs that these people must there be classed as in the Stone Age: here is a good case of people losing the useful art of metallurgy and reverting to the Stone Age.

As the idea of the three ages became diffused throughout Europe in the nineteenth century and was applied to the study of the material remains of early human culture in all parts of the continent, it became modified and elaborated.

Indeed, the northern archaeologists themselves soon recognised two divisions in the Stone Age—an Old Stone Age when only chipped stone tools were used, and a New Stone Age when the grinding and polishing of stone tools was known. Lord Avebury suggested for these two divisions of the Stone Age the terms Palaeolithic and Neolithic,[1] and so firmly established have these two subdivisions become that it is common to see references to the 'four' ages of man—the Palaeolithic, Neolithic, Bronze and Iron Ages. More recently a phase, transitional in time between the Palaeolithic and Neolithic, has been recognised, and for this Jacques de Morgan suggested the name Mesolithic,[2] although Obermaier argued that the name Epipalaeolithic more properly described the phase.[3] A phase prior to the beginning of the Palaeolithic—as defined in terms of the Chellian (or Abbevillian)—is sometimes referred to as the Eolithic. Nor were these divisions of the Stone Age enough: the Palaeolithic was divided into three phases, Lower, Middle, and Upper, and the Neolithic was divided into a Lower or Early Neolithic— the Protoneolithic of Obermaier[4]—consisting of the Campignian and the Ertebølle cultures, and an Upper, Late, or Full Neolithic including the Robenhausian (or Swiss Lake-Dwelling) phase and the Carnacian (or megalithic) phase. Montelius went further than this and divided the 'Full' Neolithic into four phases in Scandinavia.

[1] *Prehistoric Times* (1865), p. 60.
[2] *Les Premières Civilisations* (Paris, 1909), pp. 136 ff.
[3] *Fossil Man in Spain* (1924), p. 323.   [4] *Ibid.*

The metal age did not escape from these elaborations and subdivisions. A period when copper was used and not bronze was distinguished between the Neolithic and Bronze Age and variously called Eneolithic or Chalcolithic or Cyprolithic[1] or Copper Age.[2] Worsaae wanted to distinguish two phases in the Bronze Age, and so did de Mortillet who called them Morgien and Larnaudien; Otto Tischler, however, divided the Bronze Age into three phases which he called the Pile-Leubingen period, the Peccatel period, and the transition to the Iron Age. Others such as Reinecke, Montelius, Sophus Muller, and Kraft have wanted to distinguish more than three phases in the Bronze Age, but, at least in western Europe, there has been general recognition of three phases which are usually termed Early, Middle, and Late.

It was realised that man throughout the greater part of historic time in western Europe has been using iron, so the term Early or Pre-Roman Iron Age was used to distinguish that part of the Iron Age which was Pre-Roman. Worsaae tried to distinguish three phases in the Early Iron Age, while de Mortillet listed five periods which he called Hallstattien, Marnien, Lugdenien, Champdolien, and the Wabenien. Hans Hildebrand, however, distinguished

[1] Cleland, *Our Prehistoric Ancestors* (1928), p. 201.
[2] As there is considerable confusion about the use of these terms it is worth quoting de Morgan's definition of this phase: 'It is', he says, 'the cultural phase in which a few metal implements are found with neolithic remains'; there exists 'no knowledge of alloys, but only of the two metals, copper and gold' (*Prehistoric Man* (1924), p. 99).

only two phases in the Early Iron Age, an earlier and later which he termed respectively Hallstatt and La Tène, and this twofold division and these names have become very general in use. Tischler divided the La Tène period into three phases which he termed Early, Middle, and Late, and so did Déchelette who called them I, II, and III; but Reinecke distinguished four phases, A, B, C, and D. Reinecke also distinguished four phases in the Hallstatt which he also labelled A, B, C, and D; but Déchelette here found only two periods, I and II, corresponding to Reinecke's C and D.[1]

Thus the simple system of the three ages has now become elaborated into a complicated succession of Eolithic, Palaeolithic, Mesolithic, Neolithic, Chalcolithic, Bronze Age, Early Iron Age, Historic Iron Age, merging, one supposes, into an age of steel: and our text-books of prehistoric archaeology are full of forbidding tables based on subdivisions of this succession. The existence of such elaborate tables does prove beyond all cavil, were such proof needed here, that the concept of the three ages does indeed form the 'corner stone of modern archaeology' as Macalister said; but sometimes, looking at such tables or listening to archaeologists talking easily of Mesolithic II or Neolithic IV or Early Bronze Age B or La Tène I A,

[1] For a good account of the development of Iron Age subdivisions see de Navarro's Rhys Lecture (*Proc. Brit. Acad.* 1936, vol. xxii). It is worth noting here that Hawkes (*Antiquity*, 1931, pp. 60 ff.) abandons the Hallstatt and La Tène divisions in treating of the Early Iron Age in Britain and propounds a threefold division into A, B, and C.

it is a little difficult to recognise the simple division into industrial stages which Thomsen and Worsaae propounded. The complexity and formality of some of these tables makes one forget the simplicity of the idea of the three ages which underlies them. But it is not only the simplicity of the idea of the three ages which has been lost in the elaboration of these tables: in many cases the idea itself has vanished. The simple division has been so systematised and elaborated, so garnished with sub-divisions and loaded with names, that it is no longer possible to see the wood for the trees. It is inevitable that any scientific idea should be elaborated and developed, but in the case of the three ages of Thomsen the change has not merely been one of elaboration: for the three ages have now been given different connotations—cultural, chronological, racial, diffusionist, functional-economic—and they are no longer the simple industrial and technological stages which they were originally conceived to be. It is our concern here to discuss the various connotations that have been given to the three-age system, and to question whether these developments are reasonable and valid and useful.

III

1. THE TYPOLOGICAL USAGE

The basis of all prehistoric research consists in the description and distinction of archaeological types and the study of associations of these types, which, if significant

28

and persistent, we call cultures. This rather bald statement perhaps needs some elaboration here. It should not really be necessary here to define what is meant by archaeological 'types' and by archaeological 'associations', but the words are still used with a wide variety of connotations. As it seems to me, an archaeological type is merely the unit of classification of material remains and compares with the species and variety of biological classification. Thus we may find in a dwelling-place site, for instance, various objects, some of them of non-human origin, and others of human origin or fashioning, i.e. artefacts. These various artefacts may be grouped into various types such as palstaves and bone points and painted pottery. These types are said to be found in association if they are found together, and association is of two kinds, (1) original, and (2) subsequent. In the first category, i.e. original association, all the types were deposited at the same place together, that is to say, while the site was being used as a dwelling-place or while the grave was being used for burial. In a subsequent association this is not so, and the types are together for other reasons such as that they have slipped down from higher layers or that the grave or dwelling site has been subsequently re-used or that the stratigraphical sequence at a site has been disturbed by burrowing animals. An original association results in a closed find while a subsequent association results in an open find. What interests us in archaeology is the closed find, the original association, because it reveals the contemporary deposition and therefore probably contemporary usage[1] of certain artefactual types and is one of the main bases of relative chronology: this is frequently referred to not specifically as original association but just as 'association',[2] and wherever the word association is used here without the qualifying phrase 'subsequent' it should be taken to mean original association.

If there is sometimes confusion about the usage of the terms 'archaeological types' and 'association' there should surely be no two opinions as to what we mean in pre-historic archaeology by a 'culture'—it is a widespread anthropological concept and refers to a group of people who possess the same or roughly the same material, moral, and social culture. Prehistoric archaeology is, naturally, largely concerned only with the material aspect of cultural activity, as usually it is only this aspect which can safely be deduced from the material remains left to us, and therefore prehistoric cultures appear to us as little more than significant and persistent associated assemblages of artefacts. We stress the word 'appear' for, notwith-standing appearances, a prehistoric culture was very much more than its archaeological expression at the present day, although now we can usually only guess at these aspects of the vanished culture. It is as mistaken for anthropo-logists to declare that all prehistoric cultures are merely

[1] But this is not necessarily so, and it does not necessarily imply contemporary manufacture.

[2] It was thus used by Montelius in his *Die Typologische Methode* ('Die älteren Kulturperioden im Orient und in Europa, 1. Die Methode'. (Stockholm, 1903)), the classic discussion of problems of association and typology.

assemblages of artefacts as for archaeologists to pretend they can treat all prehistoric cultures as anthropologists do living ones. The exigencies of our sources prevent archaeological practice from living up to the theory of prehistory here.

The terms 'industry' and 'civilisation' are almost as variously used in prehistory as are 'culture' and 'association'. Industry is surely merely the archaeological expression of the anthropologist's 'subculture', just as the term 'complex' is the purely archaeological aspect of a culture: it is an assemblage of artefacts differing slightly from the norm of the culture but occurring sufficiently frequently to merit its being given a special name as a variant or constituent variant of a culture. An industry is a facies of a culture and a culture is an agglomeration of industries. Similarly, a culture is a facies of a civilisation: a civilisation to the student of early history is a group of cultures having certain distinct features in common. The successive groupings of our archaeological material are then: site—industry—culture—civilisation. The terms civilisation, culture, industry, having a specialised meaning here are not used in archaeology as they are in general parlance. But we digress: here our main concern is with typological nomenclature:[1] it is highly necessary that all

[1] Even the term typology is sometimes misunderstood: it implies two processes: (1) the distinction and naming of archaeological types (i.e. the classificatory and taxonomic aspect of typology); and (2) the arrangement of these types in sequences (i.e. the evolutionary aspect of typology).

archaeological types should have names by which they can always be described, and we find that it is divisions of the Thomsen three-age system that have supplied many of these names. Thus we speak of Neolithic axes, of Neolithic A and B pottery in England, and of Mesolithic flint implements. These usages are not conducive to clear thinking, for Neolithic axes (i.e. polished axes of stone) are not restricted to the Neolithic stages, while the pottery we describe in England as Neolithic A occurs in association with metal types in burial chambers in southern Iberia, and the microlithic flint types often loosely described as Mesolithic also occur in contexts varying from the Old Stone Age to the Bronze Age. The truth is that there is frequently no identity in time and in technological associations between the objects nominated with reference to these stages and the stages themselves: nor can the technological stages be defined in terms of any such objects.

2. The Cultural Usage

If cultures are, then, little more to the prehistoric archaeologist than significant and persistent associations of artefacts, the method of defining them is surely to proceed from the isolation and association of types: but much of the nineteenth century was spent not in working in this way but in subdividing the three or four technological stages into numbers of workable units and calling these 'periods' or 'cultures'. This naturally produced a single succession of cultures, and this agreed well with the evolutionary doctrines so strong at the time. Much of the research of the last twenty years has been concerned with breaking these evolutionary successions and showing that in most areas in the past several distinct and separate cultures often co-existed contemporaneously.

A few examples will illustrate this unfortunate process. The Palaeolithic in Europe was first split up, as we have seen, into Early, Middle and Late, or Lower, Middle and Upper: then the Lower Palaeolithic was divided into two phases—the first the Chellian, the second the Acheulian. The Middle Palaeolithic was not split up but was equated with the Mousterian culture, and the Upper Palaeolithic was divided into two phases, the Solutrian and the Magdalenian. In 1906 Breuil came to the conclusion that many of the flints described as Magdalenian were really earlier than the Solutrian, and at the International Congress of Anthropology and Archaeology at Monaco he proposed to call them the Aurignacian culture. This suggestion was accepted and now the succession of Palaeolithic cultures read as follows:

Upper	6. Magdalenian
	5. Solutrian
	4. Aurignacian
Middle	3. Mousterian
Lower	2. Acheulian
	1. Chellian

Such a table is to be found in any archaeological text-book

of the early twentieth century and indeed persisted up to 1920 and later.[1]

Obermaier, however, had distinguished as early as 1916 core-tool cultures and flake-tool cultures in the Lower Palaeolithic industries: Baier and Menghin developed these notions, and the Abbé Breuil now sets forth two series of cultures in what was the Lower and Middle Palaeolithic as follows:

Core-tool cultures
{ Micoquian
  Acheulian
  Chellian

Flake-tool cultures
{ Mousterian
  Levalloisian
  Clactonian
  Ipswichian

This change was partly the result of the spread of archaeological research all over the world and the realisation that the classic French sequence did not hold universally, but also the result of the realisation that in France itself this single succession was incorrect and that the story was not one of an evolutionary sequence but of independent and different cultures co-existing contemporaneously.[2]

The same thing has recently been shown to be true in the Upper Palaeolithic:[3] and in the Neolithic this has often

[1] As Childe points out (*Proc. Preh. Soc.* 1935, p. 4) the evolutionary idea still dominated the textbooks of Macalister, Burkitt, MacCurdy and Sollas published after 1920.

[2] For more complicated and detailed tables than the one quoted see the recent writings of Leakey, Wright, and Paterson.

[3] Vide D. A. E. Garrod, *Proc. Preh. Soc.* 1938, pp. 1 ff., and for a discussion of the problems of Palaeolithic classification in general see D. A. E. Garrod's papers in *Proc. Preh. Soc. East Anglia,* 1925–27.

been shown in many areas such as Britain, Switzerland, and northern Europe. In Britain there is now a general recognition that during the Neolithic in the British Isles there co-existed three groups of cultures, a southern, characterised by the Windmill Hill culture; an eastern, characterised by many cultures at present not clearly delimited but associated with Peterborough pottery, grooved pottery, rusticated pottery, and the Beaker ceramics; and a western, the Atlantic group, characterised by communal burial in chambered barrows, several of whose cultures have recently been delimited.[1] In the Neolithic of northern Europe Montelius adopted a single sequence of evolutionary phases which he numbered I, II, III, and IV, but not only is the existence of phase I now generally denied but it is also generally recognised that during phases II, III, and IV there existed—at first quite separate—three cultures, the one associated with the communal burials in chambered barrows, the second associated with the single graves and battle-axes, and the third associated with survivals of kitchen-midden 'Mesolithic' folk. In the Bronze Age the various divisions such as Early, Middle, and Late or periods I–VI have stayed longer without question, but there are strong indications that these subdivisions of the three-age system mask the real cultural divisions. In England, for instance, where we have been accustomed to speak of an Early Bronze 'culture', there probably existed a number of cultures: and recently Piggott has rendered

[1] For a summary of this delimitation see Daniel, *Proc. Preh. Soc.* 1940.

splendid service to the advancement of Bronze Age studies by isolating one of these cultures and calling it the Wessex culture.[1] It is noteworthy here that the Wessex culture does not coincide with the limits of the Early Bronze Age but laps over into the Middle Bronze Age.

The adherence to the subdivisions of the three ages and the arrangement of these subdivisions in an evolutionary 'cultural' sequence was not the only cultural misuse of the three-age system. Archaeologists, while recognising cultures on a proper artefactual basis, have yet nominated them with reference to the three-age system. Thus the culture characterised by an association of plain Western pottery, polished axes with pointed oval sections, leaf- and lozenge-shaped arrowheads, antler combs, serrated flint flakes or saws, pottery spoons or ladles, carved objects of chalk, and causewayed or interrupted-ditch camps, and found on the downs of Wiltshire, Hampshire, Dorset, and Sussex, has been labelled not the Windmill Hill culture from its first completely excavated type-site[2] but the Neolithic A culture—a name already used for a group of prehistoric British pottery; and both uses prejudice the chronological and technological status of the culture and prejudge it in the eyes of comparative archaeologists.

We have already mentioned Hawkes's pioneer attempts

---

[1] Piggott, *Proc. Preh. Soc.* 1938, pp. 52 ff. Hencken (*Archaeology of Cornwall* (1932)) appears to distinguish a south-western or Cornish culture of this period.

[2] It is good to know that some archaeologists do refer to this culture as the Windmill Hill culture.

to break away from the Hallstatt I and II and La Tène I, II, III, and IV classification of the Iron Age and to classify the Early Iron Age in Britain on a new basis. This classification has been subsequently modified by Hawkes himself and by Ralegh Radford, Wheeler, and Ward-Perkins; between them they distinguish at present eight cultures as follows:[1]

(1) Confined to east and south-east England (e.g. Castle Hill, Scarborough, Park Brow, Findon Park), beginning in the fifth or late sixth centuries B.C. and derived from the Lower Rhine area.

(2) In the Wessex area (e.g. All Cannings Cross and Hengistbury Head) a culture derived from the Jogassiens of the Marne area and beginning about 500–450 B.C.

(3) A culture in the north-east and east of England, especially Yorkshire and the Wash area (Lincolnshire, Cambridgeshire, and Norfolk), derived directly from the Paris region about 300–250 B.C.

(4) Centred in Cornwall (e.g. Chun) and characterised by round hill-forts, courtyard houses, and the stamped-duck motif on pottery, and derived from Brittany or Spain.

(5) Found in Somerset and best known by the celebrated lake-villages of Glastonbury and Meare and best remembered by the magnificent curvilinear decorated pottery reminiscent of Breton pots, such as at Plouhinec and St-Pol-de-Léon.

[1] As Ward-Perkins says (*Proc. Preh. Soc.* 1938, p. 156) it may well be that yet more cultures of this period await recognition.

(6) Centred in the hill-forts of Wessex (e.g. Maiden Castle).

(7) At present the least understood of these eight cultures but distinguished in south-eastern Britain by Ward-Perkins on the basis of the omphalos-bowls.[1]

(8) The Aylesford-Swarling-Welwyn group concentrated in north Kent, Essex, Hertfordshire, south Cambridgeshire, and south Bedfordshire and derived from the country south of the Ardennes at about 75 B.C. This group gives continuity with the Belgae of historic times.[2]

The isolation and description of these cultures is a fine piece of research, but its value is considerably lessened by the fact that these cultures instead of being given straightforward geographical or type-site names, such as the Cornish culture, the Glastonbury culture, the Aylesford culture, have been grouped together in a curious way, the first two as Iron Age A, the next five as Iron Age B and the last as Iron Age C, and the individual cultures named in a cumbersome way with reference to this grouping as Iron Age B (north-eastern) and so forth. I can see no conceivable advantage achieved by naming these cultures with reference to the three-age system, and it is noteworthy that in his fine analysis of the Scottish Iron Age, Professor Childe, our chief British exponent of scientific methodology in prehistoric archaeology, refers to his

[1] *Proc. Preh. Soc.* 1938, pp. 151 ff.

[2] Hawkes and Dunning argued for a ninth culture—a second Belgic invasion of Britain. On this see de Navarro, *op. cit.* pp. 22-3.

newly defined cultures not by names derived from the three-age system but by independent names such as the Abernethy and Castle cultures.[1]

Our argument here is briefly this: (1) cultures should be built up from a study of persistent associations of archaeological types and not arrived at by splitting up a preconceived grouping of human remains; (2) two or more cultures may co-exist contemporaneously in one region; (3) cultures frequently outstep the three-age system, and their beginnings or endings do not coincide with these stages. There is much dispute whether the Beaker cultures in England should be Neolithic or Early Bronze Age; but the facts are surely that the Beaker folk were first technically Neolithic and gradually learnt the arts of metallurgy in Britain. The naming of cultures then by parts of the three-age system and the splitting up of the three-age system into smaller units and labelling them cultures seems to me to dispense with the *impedimenta* of scientific method in cultural diagnosis, and there appears to be no good authority for this dispensation.

3. THE CHRONOLOGICAL USAGE

The three ages and their subdivisions are at present very widely used not only for typological nomenclature and for cultural classification and nomenclature but also for chronological purposes: objects, cultures, peoples are 'dated' to the Early Bronze Age or the Late Mesolithic.

[1] *The Prehistory of Scotland* (1935), pp. 236 ff.

There can be no question that the three ages are primarily industrial and technological phases: of what value can they be chronologically? Clearly these phases have a temporal existence so that it is possible to date an artefact or culture to the Bronze Age, if we mean that such an artefact was in use or that such a culture was flourishing when bronze and stone, but no iron, were used by man for the manufacture of his weapons and implements. But to say that a bronze axe, for example, belongs to the Bronze Age, is almost saying no more than that it is made of bronze, which is perilously near saying nothing at all.

Little detailed chronological significance can be attributed to these ages because they were not everywhere contemporaneous. This fact should be obvious from the nature of the spread of these phases, and the early archaeologists realised the chronological limitations of the concept, as we have mentioned above. 'Such a classification into different ages in no way implies any exact chronology,' declared Evans, 'far less one applicable to all countries of Europe alike, but it is to be regarded as significant of a succession of different stages of civilisation.'[1] 'The Stone period is regarded by many as a mere measure of time...', wrote Stevens: 'It cannot, however, be too often repeated that the Stone Period, as a whole, does not afford a measure of time. The Stone Period is a thing of the present as well as of the past, it exists to-day in some countries, it is actually being watched as it expires in others—and it existed elsewhere thousands of years since.'[2] Recent

[1] *Ancient Stone Implements*, p. 2. [2] *Arch. Journ.* 1872, p. 393.

writers have re-emphasised this point: Childe declares 'the several ages did not begin nor end simultaneously all over the world',[1] and Piggott says, 'there are a great many Bronze Ages—one for each region, in fact—and the beginnings and end of them are obviously rather vague and not necessarily the same in any two regions'.[2]

Let us labour this point with some examples. The Early Iron Age began in Asia Minor about 1200 B.C., in Italy about 1000 B.C., in central Europe about 900 B.C., in China about 700 B.C., in southern England about 600 B.C., in Japan about A.D. 200 and in Fiji during Baron von Hügel's visits to those islands in the 1870's. Childe chooses the Neolithic as his example and points out that both the Tasians who dwelt in Egypt about 5000 B.C. and the Maoris of the eighteenth century in New Zealand must, from the point of view of the three-age system, be classed as Neolithic: he comments very properly that, 'a period which telescopes into nothingness the whole of written history is useless as a chronological period'.[3] The various ages of the Thomsen system are homotaxial rather than contemporaneous: a glance at a chronological table such as that of Burkitt and Childe,[4] or that in Furon's *Manuel de Préhistoire Générale*,[5] will reveal the extent of this homotaxy.

But while it may be conceded that on a world-wide

[1] *Man Makes Himself*, p. 49.
[2] *The Progress of Early Man* (1938), p. 24.
[3] *Proc. Preh. Soc.* 1935, p. 2.   [4] *Antiquity*, June 1932.
[5] Table II, pp. 392–3.

basis the three ages do not provide an accurate or useful chronological system, many have argued that in small areas the system of the three ages and their divisions has a chronological value, and that by the Early Bronze Age in Glamorgan or the Early Iron Age in Wessex we signify an accurate period of time. This is no doubt true, but the essence of chronology is that it must be objective and applicable over a fairly wide area. The British Isles is an area sufficiently small for us to expect a uniform basis for our chronology there; yet of what use chronologically can be a system which makes it possible for a point in prehistoric time to be described as Early Iron Age in Sussex, Bronze Age in Wales, and Stone Age, say, in the Orkneys?

The detailed subdivisions have, of course, been approximately dated in certain regions: thus the Hallstatt phase of the Early Iron Age in central Europe is dated from 850 or 900 to 450 B.C. It might be argued that the expression 'Hallstatt' when used for dating in France and Britain then meant not the first half of the Early Iron Age in those regions but the period 900 or 850 to 450 B.C., and that these phases had now merely become convenient names for approximately dated periods. If this were so it would be deplorably inconvenient because these terms had already other and more proper connotations: but it is even not so—we do date the Early Bronze Age in Italy, in Spain, in Bohemia and in Britain differently and we do not understand by this phrase the period say from 1900 to 1500 B.C. in all these areas. We do not use the three-age system as we use the term Roman period for the first to fourth Christian centuries even in areas such as Ireland, north Scotland and Scandinavia where the Romans never were. Dr Mahr has protested strongly against 'the indiscriminate ascription of "Hallstatt period", "Early Iron Age", and other "Ages" and cultural "periods" to parts of Europe where these regional terms cease to have any very real chronological significance'.[1] As Childe stresses, the three ages and their divisions cannot possibly survive 'as designations of true periods of time which could be expressed in terms of solar years in our calendar'.[2]

The test of any chronological scheme is surely its applicability: does the three-age system in fact work as a time scheme? One example will suffice: let us take the chambered barrows of southern Britain as an example of the loose thinking that often exists on the chronological value of these ages. One is always being asked whether the burial chambers are Early Neolithic, Late Neolithic, or Early Bronze Age or even later in 'date'. What reply can be made to this query? Only one or two of the burial chambers yield metal in primary association, so that it is fair to say that they all belong to the industrial phase represented by the later part of the Stone Age; but there is no doubt that while many of them are contemporary with other south British cultures which are in the same phase of industrial development, many others were built and used until perhaps the middle of the second millen-

[1] *Proc. Preh. Soc.* 1937, pp. 278–80.
[2] *Proc. Preh. Soc.* 1935, p. 7.

nium B.C. when effective cultures in the Bronze Age were flourishing in southern Britain. To what phase, then, must these cultures be 'dated'? The truth is that it is impossible to 'date' them to a phase in the three-age system, and herein perhaps lies the impossibility of using the three ages as a chronological framework, even in a small area like southern Britain.

We have previously referred to the 'dating' of the Beakers in Great Britain in terms of the three-age system. Childe, in studying the Scottish cultures characterised by chambered barrows and by Beakers, has fully realised the implications of trying to fit in these cultures with any of the cultural or chronological usages of the three-age system. He summarises the difficulties in a passage which we may be forgiven for quoting in full here as it admirably stresses our argument in the foregoing pages. 'No metal objects have ever been found with the original burials in collective tombs in the British Isles', he declares,[1] 'and hence these structures are generally referred to a "Neo-lithic" period. Objects of copper or bronze do accompany Beakers, and individual interments in short cists are accordingly commonly assigned to the "Bronze Age". But this contrast may be due to a difference in economic organisation or in piety rather than to a distinction in age. In Scotland few individual interments have been accompanied by metal objects and those that have are often

[1] *Prehistory of Scotland*, pp. 22–3. This statement is not quite correct, for bronze was found at Obadiah's Barrow in the Isles of Scilly.

44

marked as relatively late by the character of their pottery. On the other hand, collective tombs contain stone implements that, as near as Yorkshire, have been found associated with bronze weapons in individual graves. To this extent the current use of the terms Neolithic and Bronze Age seems frankly misleading.'

4. THE FUNCTIONAL-ECONOMIC USAGE

Recently Childe, while recognising the inapplicability of many of the usages of the three-age system which we have already discussed, has put forward a new interpretation of Thomsen's ages which he calls 'the functional-economic interpretation'. 'I would suggest', he writes, 'that the terms palaeolithic, neolithic, etc., should be regarded as indicative of economic stages'[1]...'the classification Old Stone Age, New Stone Age, Bronze Age and Iron Age draws attention to real revolutions that affected all departments of human life.'[2] The three ages, he says, may now 'be given a profound significance as indicating vital stages in human progress'.[2] Elsewhere Childe writes 'the archaeologist's ages correspond roughly to economic stages. Each new "age" is ushered in by an economic revolution of the same kind and having the same effect as the "Industrial Revolution" of the eighteenth century.'[3] Others have, at various times, argued in much the same way: Hodder Westropp, for instance, equated the Palaeo-

[1] *Proc. Preh. Soc.* 1935, p. 9.   [2] *Ibid.* p. 7.
[3] *Man Makes Himself*, p. 39.

lithic with the hunting phase of man's existence, the Neolithic with the herdsman phase, and the Bronze Age with the beginning of agricultural pursuits;[1] and Miss Collum has stressed that the Thomsen ages 'have a social and economic rather than a chronological indication';[2] but no one has argued the case so fully and cogently as Childe.

It was the late Sir Grafton Elliot Smith who first insisted on the division of human history into two stages, the one characterised by food gatherers, the second and later by food producers. This idea has been developed by Perry, by Peake and Fleure, and by Childe, and there can be no doubt that the change from a food-gathering economy to one based on food production was one of the major revolutions in the history of man: it is sometimes known as the First Economic Revolution or the Food-Producing Revolution. Childe suggests that there were two other revolutions within the food-producing stage: the first that which developed the city, specialisation of labour, and the beginnings of regular foreign trade which he calls the Urban Revolution; and the second which is generally known as the Industrial Revolution, though it is no greater a revolution in industry than the food-producing one or the urban one.[3] The Industrial Revolution

[1] *Pre-Historic Phases*, 1872. Of course the existence of the last two of these phases—the herding and agricultural—in the order given is now questioned.

[2] *The Iron Age Megalithic Monument at Tressé* (1935).

[3] These are sometimes known as the second and third economic revolutions.

does not concern us here: its historical position is fixed, as also its relation to the Thomsen system of the three ages—it is an incident in the Later Iron Age, unless it might be claimed to have started a new age—the Age of Steel and Power Tools. It is the relation of the other two revolutions to the three-age system that is of great interest to us.

Peake suggested equating the Food-Producing Revolution with the beginning of the Neolithic Age;[1] Vayson de Pradenne[2] and Childe have adopted this equation. Childe wishes further to equate the Urban Revolution with other of the Thomsen ages: he argues that in the Near East the beginning of the Urban Revolution coincides with the Bronze Age,[3] and that 'particularly in Europe, probably also in tropical countries, the discovery of an economical process for producing iron in quantity—that is the mark of the Iron Age—had a similar result'.[4] Thus Childe equates the economic revolutions which undoubtedly existed with Thomsen's system of technological stages: this, in brief, is the essential of his functional-economic interpretation.

We are not criticising here the truth of these economic revolutions: as Childe sets them out they are the facts of human history in the sphere of economic development:[5]

[1] *Journ. Roy. Anth. Inst.* LVII, pp. 22 ff.   [2] *Antiquity*, 1935, p. 309.
[3] See *Man Makes Himself*, Chap. VII, 'The Urban Revolution'.
[4] *Man Makes Himself*, p. 41.
[5] Piggott (*Progress of Early Man*) has an even simpler scheme whereby he divides man's economic existence into three phases: (1) Man the Hunter, (2) Man the Farmer, (3) Man the Mechanic.

we merely question their equation with Thomsen's stages and the naming of some of them by terms borrowed from the Thomsen system. Our criticism of the equation is twofold: (1) in the first place, as Childe himself frankly admits, the Second Revolution corresponds in one part of the world with the Bronze Age and in another with the Iron Age;[1] (2) in the second place the Food-Producing Revolution does not correspond exactly with the Neolithic stage: many of the very earliest food-producing cultures should perhaps be more properly described as Chalcolithic. Nevertheless, it is generally true that the change from food-gathering to food-producing is to be correlated with the beginning of the Neolithic. Even so, to equate the First Economic Revolution with the change from the Mesolithic to the Neolithic does not mean that the two systems—the functional-economic stages and the Thomsen technological stages—are identical; nor does it make it any more convenient to call them both by the same name: they remain separate and different groupings of human history—the one technological, the other functional-economic.

5. OTHER USAGES

Many other interpretations have been forced on the three-age system other than the four most important ones already discussed. Very common in books such as those

[1] Or more probably with the Late Bronze Age.

of Rice Holmes[1] is what may be called the ethnic or diffusionist interpretation of the three-age system: this is the reverse of T. E. Peet's notions already mentioned.[2] Rice Holmes and many of his contemporaries conceived of each age as being heralded by a great invasion, and their works are full of Neolithic invasions, and Bronze Age invasions, and Early Iron Age invasions. All this has been shown to be fallacious—each technological stage was not necessarily introduced to a region by invasion but often by trade or the peaceful penetration of travelling smiths; and many very notable ethnic movements occurred within the ages of the three-age system.[3] Perhaps as a result of these cataclysmic notions of the origin of the three ages, and partly as a result of the notions commonly held thirty to fifty years ago about the nature of races, each age was often conceived of in terms of physical anthropology, and much of the analyses of prehistoric man made by competent anatomists and anthropometricians has been ruined by talk of the Neolithic Race and the Bronze Age Race and so forth. These two misconceptions have probably died out by now from scientific writings and they need not detain us here,[4] any

[1] *Ancient Britain and the Invasions of Julius Caesar* (1907).

[2] *Vide supra*, p. 23.

[3] For the strength of the ethnic interpretation of the three ages cf. the first suggestion by Crawford in 1922 (*Ant. Journ.* 1922, pp. 27 ff.) of a Late Bronze Age invasion.

[4] I may be taking too optimistic a view of the death of these misconceptions. Certainly they do still occur in the writings of Morant, Hooke and Martin.

more than should Childe's suggestion that 'the criteria used by archaeologists to distinguish his several "ages" serve also as indexes to the state of science'.[1]

It is sometimes argued that even if the three-age system is valueless from the point of view of typological, cultural, chronological and functional-economic classification and nomenclature, at least the major divisions of the system do mark out suitable and significant groupings of human cultures—that they are important stages in human development even if they are not functional-economic stages. But this view is open to question. There is a great break in the Old Stone Age between the core-tool and flake-tool cultures of what used to be called the Lower and Middle Palaeolithic on the one hand, and the backed blade and burin industries of the Upper Palaeolithic on the other. Elliot Smith realised this break in his study of the physical remains and proposed the names Palaeanthropic and Neanthropic to distinguish the two phases.[2] Jacques de Morgan reserved the word Palaeolithic for the earlier cultures and proposed the term Archaeolithic for the cultures formerly known as Upper Palaeolithic.[3] Menghin went further and grouped the Upper Palaeolithic and Mesolithic to form one group which he termed the Miolithic: calling all that went before the Protolithic.[4]

---

[1] *Man Makes Himself*, p. 39. [2] *Proc. Brit. Academy*, VII, p. 9.
[3] *Prehistoric Man* (1924), Chap. II.
[4] *Weltgeschichte der Steinzeit*. In a review of this work (*Ant. Journ.* 1930, p. 296) Childe characterised Menghin as abandoning 'the terms palaeolithic, mesolithic, neolithic, etc., which are currently applied

Spinden agrees with this view and declares, 'Menghin is right...in his insistence that one order of man's cultural evolution ended with the Mousterian and that the upper Palaeolithic and Mesolithic should be combined to make a second one'.[1] As we have already mentioned, in many parts of the world it is difficult to know whether the first food-producing cultures are to be classed as Neolithic or Chalcolithic, and in all areas the Neolithic cultures and those of the earliest metal age are very closely akin. Kendrick realised this clearly in 1925 and suggested for Britain the use of the term 'Eochalcic Episode' for the period usually known as the Neolithic and Early Bronze Age—a splendid suggestion that never should have been forgotten.[2] In central and northern Europe there is no great break at the beginning of the Bronze Age but rather at the beginning of the Late Bronze Age: the period from the beginning of the Late Bronze until the Roman period may very properly be treated as a whole. It is significant that Childe in his *Dawn of European Civilisation*, and Hawkes in his recent *Prehistoric Foundations of Europe*, both bring their books to an end in the Middle Bronze Age and thus implicitly recognise that the period 1400–1000 marks a new stage in European history. Indeed, while it is not our object to propose any new classifications, we cannot but point out that the right-hand column of the

on the basis of other superficial criteria and may be ambiguously used as denoting either chronological divisions or cultural grades'.

[1] *Early Man* (ed. MacCurdy), pp. 107, 109.
[2] T. D. Kendrick, *The Axe Age* (1925), Chap. VII.

following table is as significant a grouping of human cultures, or even a more significant grouping, than that on the left-hand which is the Thomsen three-age system.

Early Iron Age La Tène Hallstatt	Full prehistoric Metal Age
Bronze Age Late Middle Early	Eochalcic Episode or Age
Chalcolithic	
Neolithic	
Mesolithic	Miolithic
Palaeolithic Upper Middle Lower	Protolithic

IV

We can now summarise briefly the argument of this paper. The Thomsen system of the three ages of man was established in the early nineteenth century as a result of classifying the material in the National Museum at Copenhagen, and the truth of the system was proved empirically by Danish archaeologists in the field. The ages are really three technological stages, and their applicability only extends to Europe, the Near East and large parts of Asia: elsewhere, e.g. in Africa and Oceania, man has lived through only two technological stages—the Stone Age and the Iron Age, and in many parts he is still in the first stage—the Stone Age. The nomenclature and divisions of these technological stages have been extended to other classifications of mankind, and they have been reinterpreted in many new ways: so much so that it is the custom at the present day to define the Neolithic, for example, on four criteria—agriculture, domestication of animals, pottery, and polished stone tools. We cannot state too clearly that the only criterion of the Neolithic properly speaking (i.e. as Avebury defined it) is the presence of polished stone tools: there should be no question that the three ages and their divisions are still primarily technological stages. None of their reinterpretations is accurate, or justified, and even if they were, it would be a source of great confusion to use the same set of terms for technological stages, for artefacts, for cultures, for chronology, for the functional-economic periods and even for other purposes. Our first duty, then, if we persist in using the three-age terms in a chronological and cultural sense, is to distinguish between these usages and the correct use of these terms for the technological stages they properly describe. Macalister declared: 'It would avoid an undeniable ambiguity if we were to speak of the Stages rather than of the Ages of Civilisation, but the latter term has become so well established that nothing but confusion would result from disturbing it.'[1] In my opinion little short of confusion has resulted from not disturbing it: by all means let us refer to the Thomsen technological ages as stages if we are retaining the terms Bronze Age, Early Iron Age, etc., to describe cultures and chronology. That is the very least we can do: those who do not I suspect, in Housman's phrase, 'of calling in ambiguity of language to promote confusion of thought'.[2]

But this is not really enough: we should abandon terms derived from the three-age system for our descriptions of artefacts and cultures and chronology. It is, of course, easy to be destructively critical of an existing system or practice: even very little and very stupid children can throw stones at old men and telegraph poles. It may be asked what can we do for artefactual, cultural, chronological divisions and nomenclature if the three-age system is restricted to its proper and pristine usage? Artefacts can and should be named by descriptive terms (e.g. backed blade, polished stone axe-head, palstave, leaf-shaped sword), by terms derived from type-sites (e.g. Mörigen sword, Deverel-Rimbury pottery, Peterborough pottery), or by general regional names (e.g. Western pottery, Irish bronze axes). Cultures too should be given geographical names (e.g. Wessex culture, Cornish culture, Apennine culture, Perigordian), or names from type-sites (e.g. Glastonbury

---

[1] *Textbook of European Archaeology*, I, p. 11.

[2] A. E. Housman, *The Name and Nature of Poetry* (Cambridge, 1933), p. 31.

culture, Windmill Hill culture, La Tène culture), or even —though this is less satisfactory to my mind—names derived from type-objects (e.g. Chatelperronian, Gravettian, the Separate-Grave culture). The functional-economic revolutions can still be termed the Food-Producing Revolution and the Urban Revolution.

Chronology is perhaps the most difficult problem, but it is also the most pressing, because the basis of our chronology must be objective. Geology should form the framework of our chronology from the earliest appearance of man to the end of the Pleistocene. Within this range the terms Late Pliocene, Middle Pleistocene and so forth will suffice, or can be replaced by more accurate terms based on glacial and pluvial phenomena. In a recent number of *Nature*,[1] Paterson has set forth a table of the Pleistocene showing it divided into Lower, Middle and Upper periods with more detailed subdivisions as L_1 and L_2, M_1 and M_2, and U_1, U_2 and U_3: this surely forms a first-rate framework for early human chronology. The end of phase U_3—the end of the Ice Age—is usually dated at about 8300 B.C., and from that time to the present day is generally known as the Holocene or Recent Period. For convenience of reference this could be divided into seven periods as follows: I, 8300–6800 B.C.; II, 6800–5000 B.C.; III, 5000–3000 B.C.; IV, 3000–1500 B.C.; V, 1500–1 B.C.; VI, 1 B.C. to A.D. 1000; and VII, A.D. 1000 to the present day. Clark uses the first three of these periods in his detailed studies of the Mesolithic or Epipalaeolithic

[1] *Nature*, 6 July 1940, pp. 12 ff. and table, p. 13.

cultures of northern Europe, but he refers to these periods
not in an objective way as Holocene I, II, III, etc., but as
Mesolithic I, II, and III.[1]

In most regions of the world an exact chronology based
on human records can be established at some date in the
Holocene, and the necessity of preserving the divisions of
the Holocene then ceases: in America this comes in
A.D. 1492, in Britain at 55 B.C., but in Egypt and Meso-
potamia at some date in the fourth millennium B.C. In
Britain, though we have no exact dates before 55 B.C., we
can get approximate dates tied across to Egyptian and
Mesopotamian chronology as far back as about 2500 B.C.
From the end of Holocene III in Britain until 55 B.C. our
chronology could be (1) based on these approximately
fixed dates; (2) by means of approximately named
approximately dated periods; thus the period from the
end of Holocene III could be divided into a number
of periods approximately dated 3000–2500 B.C., 2500–
2100 B.C., 2100–1800 B.C., etc., and these periods given
objective labels or names;[2] (3) by means of a series of
sequence dates we could give the sequence date of 30 to
the end of the Holocene III, and that of 0 to the year
1 B.C. (i.e. the end of Holocene V), and all dates in between

[1] See J. G. D. Clark, *The Mesolithic Settlement of Northern Europe*
(1936), especially Chap. I.
[2] Childe has adopted this method in his *Prehistoric Communities of
the British Isles*, published since this paper was written. *Vide* pp. 7–11
of that work, where he suggests a framework of nine periods from
3000 B.C. to the Roman Conquest and gives them Roman numerals
from I to IX.

could be described with reference to this sequence. Thus if we dated the B Beaker invasion of eastern Britain as S.D. 18 this would indicate accurately its relative position in the prehistoric chronology of southern Britain without declaring that it was dated 1800 B.C., and if the exact date was subsequently found by future research to be 1500 B.C. and all our prehistoric dates too generous, the relative positions of the sequence dates would remain correct.

It is not our object here to develop these ideas, but merely to draw attention to the inadequacies of the extensions of the Thomsen system. We are just making a plea for clear thinking: it should surely be enough to label a culture Abbevillian, to say its characteristic tools are handaxes, and that it is dated to the Middle Pleistocene; or to take another example, it should be enough to name a culture the Severn-Cotswold, to say it is characterised by transepted gallery graves and by laterally chambered long barrows, and date it approximately at 2200–1800 B.C. I cannot see that any further information of value is conveyed by describing the Abbevillian as Lower Palaeolithic or debating whether the Severn-Cotswold is a Neolithic, a Chalcolithic or an Early Bronze Age culture. We are not criticising the Thomsen system: merely its misuse. The Thomsen three-age system remains a generalisation about the technical development of man, and, to my mind, it must be admitted that it is a generalisation which, at the present day, assumes little importance when compared with other generalisations such as those of the functional-economic scheme. Its importance to modern archaeologists lies in the fact that it did produce some order out of the chaos which was prehistory up to the beginning of the nineteenth century, and that it did give prehistorians something to work on, a basis for their speculations. It is in this sense that we may re-echo Macalister's description of the system as 'the corner-stone of modern archaeology'. It *has* been the corner stone, the foundation stone of modern archaeology: it was not Thomsen's fault if most subsequent archaeologists slavishly built all their structures on this one foundation stone.

An interesting parallel to the misuse of the Thomsen system comes from English architectural history. The terms Early English, Decorated, Renascence, etc., were first designed to denote architectural styles, but they have been loosely applied not as a typological and cultural criterion but to date buildings, and have even been used to date buildings not of the style so named. This has led to great confusion in dealing with contemporary buildings of different styles: and architectural historians are now retaining these names for the styles and replacing them by chronological terms for dating purposes. This is precisely what is required in prehistoric archaeology.

The development of a science appears to go through four stages: the first one of brilliant generalisation, the second one of dull development, the third one in which the facts are reviewed again and the generalisations checked and put on a new basis, and the fourth in which the science proceeds on its newly verified and corrected bases to fresh and detailed researches.[1] Thomsen's generalisation was perhaps the most brilliant in the first stage of the development of prehistoric archaeology. Since the first half of the nineteenth century we have been in the middle ages of prehistoric development—ages of dull, pedestrian specialisation with the development and division of the three-age system as an answer to all archaeological problems. We are only now beginning to climb out of this second stage of the development of prehistoric science. Boswell has declared that the present is the Golden Age of prehistoric research,[2] and de Navarro describes it as the heroic age of archaeology.[3] I wonder if these phrases are really justified? Admittedly great discoveries have been made in the last thirty years, and the development of a completely new technique—that of air photography—is one of the most spectacular advances in archaeology. And again, as we are never tired of declaring, we are scientific archaeologists; but every generation of archaeologists will describe itself as scientific and its predecessors as un-scientific bunglers, and the archaeologists of the future will be as contemptuous of our excavational methods as we are of those of Greenwell and Bateman and Mortimer —those 'hoggings' which provided us with such a great deal of valuable information.[4] We cannot justify our

[1] Hooton has well described these stages in his *Apes, Men and Morons* (1938).   [2] *Proc. Preh. Soc.* 1936, p. 149.

[3] *Op. cit.*, pp. 24–5.

[4] Although admittedly, as Crawford points out to me, they destroyed much valuable information also.

claim to be scientific at present unless, together with our technical advances and our accumulation of new data, there goes a new critical appreciation of the method and nature of archaeological science. It remains painfully true that the writings on prehistoric methodology are astonishingly few: Crawford's *Man and his Past*, Petrie's *Methods and Aims in Archaeology*, Childe's *Changing Methods and Aims in Prehistory*,[1] and Clark's *Archaeology and Society* readily spring to mind—all first-rate studies, but there is very little else on the subject in English. If our golden age of heroes in archaeology is not to become a gilt one of microtomic specialists we must pay more attention to methodology, we must review again all our facts, check all the early generalisations, and set our subject firmly on true foundations. This article has merely attempted to re-assess one of these generalisations—that of the Thomsen system of the three ages. This system has indeed been the foundation stone of modern archaeology; it is for us to say whether it is to become a mill-stone hanging around the necks of future archaeologists.

[1] *Proc. Preh. Soc.* 1935, pp. 1 ff., his Presidential Address already referred to many times throughout this article.